SONGS OF UNREASON

Books by Jim Harrison

Jim Harrison
Songs of Unreason

Copper Canyon Press
Port Townsend, Washington

Cover art: Russell Chatham, *Summer Storm,* 1998. Lithograph 16" × 20".

"Suite of Unreason" appeared in *Narrative.* "Blue" and "René Char 11" appeared in *New Poets of the American West* (Many Voices Press). "Sunlight" appeared in *Reflections* (Yale Divinity School).

Copper Canyon Press is in residence at Fort Worden State Park in Port Townsend, Washington, under the auspices of Centrum. Centrum is a gathering place for artists and creative thinkers from around the world, students of all ages and backgrounds, and audiences seeking extraordinary cultural enrichment.

LIBRARY OF CONGRESS CATALOGING-IN-PUBLICATION DATA

Harrison, Jim, 1937–

Songs of unreason / Jim Harrison.

 p. cm.

ISBN 978-1-55659-390-1 (softcover)

1. Title.

PS3558.A67S66 2011

811'.54 — dc23

2011025560

Copper Canyon Press

Post Office Box 271

Port Townsend, Washington 98368

www.coppercanyonpress.org

for Will Hearst

Life never answers.
It has no ears and doesn't hear us;
it doesn't speak, it has no tongue.
It neither goes nor stays:
we are the ones who speak,
the ones who go,
while we hear from echo to echo, year to year,
our words rolling through a tunnel with no end.
That which we call life
hears itself within us, speaks with our tongues,
and through us, knows itself.

— OCTAVIO PAZ, FROM
"RESPONSE AND RECONCILIATION,"
TRANSLATED BY ELIOT WEINBERGER

Contents

*Stanzas for the long poem "Suite of Unreason" appear on the unnumbered left-hand pages and are printed in Legato, a sans serif typeface.

SONGS OF UNREASON

BROOM

To remember you're alive
visit the cemetery of your father
at noon after you've made love
and are still wrapped in a mammalian
odor that you are forced to cherish.
Under each stone is someone's inevitable
surprise, the unexpected death
of their biology that struggled hard, as it must.
Now to home without looking back,
enough is enough.
En route buy the best wine
you can afford and a dozen stiff brooms.
Have a few swallows then throw the furniture
out the window and begin sweeping.
Sweep until the walls are
bare of paint and at your feet sweep
until the floor disappears. Finish the wine
in this field of air, return to the cemetery
in evening and wind through the stones
a slow dance of your name visible only to birds.

SUITE OF UNREASON

Nearly all my life I've noted that some of my thinking was atavistic, primitive, totemistic. This can be disturbing to one fairly learned. In this suite I wanted to examine this phenomenon.

The moon is under suspicion.
Of what use is it?
It exudes its white smoke of light.

They say the years are layers, laminae.
They lie. Our minds aren't stuck together
like trees. We're much nearer to a ball of snakes
in winter, a flock of blackbirds, a school of fish.
Your brain guides you away from sentences.
It is consoled by the odor of the chokecherry tree
that drifts its sweetness through the studio window.
Chokecherry trees have always been there
along with crab apples. The brain doesn't care
about layers. It is both vertical and horizontal
in a split second, in all directions at once.
Nearly everything we are taught is false
except how to read. All these poems that drift
upward in our free-floating minds hang there
like stationary birds with a few astonishing
girls and women. Einstein lights a cigarette
and travels beyond the galaxies that have
no layers. Our neurons are designed after 90 billion galaxies.
As a shattered teenager I struggled to paint
a copy of El Greco's *View of Toledo* to Berlioz's Requiem.
The canvas was too short but very deep. I walked
on my knees to see what the world looked like
to Toulouse-Lautrec. It didn't work. I became seven
again. It was World War II. I was about
to lose an eye. The future was still in the sky
above me, which I had to learn to capture
in the years that never learned as clouds
to be layered. First warm day. Chokecherry burst. Its song.

, , ,

Her name was imponderable.
Sitting in the grass seven feet
from the lilacs she knew
she'd never have a lover.
She tends to her knitting
which is the night.

AMERICAN SERMON

I am uniquely privileged to be alive
or so they say. I have asked others
who are unsure, especially the man with three
kids who's being foreclosed next month.
One daughter says she isn't leaving the farm,
they can pry her out with tractor
and chain. Mother needs heart surgery
but there is no insurance. A lifetime of cooking
with pork fat. My friend Sam has made
five hundred bucks in 40 years
of writing poetry. He has applied for 120
grants but so have 50,000 others. Sam keeps
strict track. The fact is he's not very good.
Back to the girl on the farm. She's been
keeping records of all the wildflowers
on the never-tilled land down the road,
a 40-acre clearing where they've bloomed
since the glaciers. She picks wild strawberries
with a young female bear who eats them. She's being
taken from the eastern Upper Peninsula down
to Lansing where Dad has a job in a
bottling plant. She won't survive the move.

′ ′ ′

That morning the sun forgot to rise
and for a while no one noticed
except a few farmers, who shot themselves.

It's better to start walking before you're born.
As with dancing you have to learn the steps
and after that free-form can be the best.
Stevens said technique is the proof of seriousness,
though the grace of a Maserati is limited to itself.
There is a human wildness held beneath the skin
that finds all barriers brutishly unbearable.
I can't walk in the shoes cobbled for me.
They weren't devised by poets but by shoemakers.

＇ ＇ ＇

The girl near the Théâtre de l'Odéon
walked so swiftly
we were astonished.

BIRD'S-EYE VIEW

In the Sandhills of Nebraska
the towns are mere islands, sandspits,
in the ocean of land while in the Upper Peninsula
of Michigan, the towns seem not very successful
attempts to hold back the forest. In Montana
the mountains are so dominant that some days
the people refuse to look at them as children
turn away from the fathers who beat them.
But of course in most places the people
have won, the cities and highways have won.
As in nearly all wars both sides have lost
and the damage follows until the end of our time.
It seems strange that it could have been done well.
Greed has always fouled our vast nest.
Tiring of language, the mind takes flight
swimming off into the ocean of air thinking
who am I that the gods and men have disappointed me?
You walk through doorways in the mind you can't walk out
then one day you discover that you've learned to fly.
From up here the water is still blue, the grass green
and the wind that buoys me is 12 billion years old.

, , ,

The fish with the huge tumor
jumped higher than my head
from my hand when released.

POET WARNING

He went to sea
in a thimble of poetry
without sail or oars
or anchor. What chance
do I have, he thought?
Hundreds of thousands
of moons have drowned out here
and there are no gravestones.

'''

The girl in the green dress
sang a wordless carol
on the yellow school bus.

I took the train from Seville to Granada with a vintner friend. I had been reading Federico García Lorca for over fifty years and needed to see where he was murdered on the mountainside near Granada. Beware old man! We visited the site of the murder, drank a little wine, and I began to drown in melancholy. We went to our hotel where I planned to stay in Lorca's room but it frightened me and I moved to another. We toured the city in the morning and I stared at the Sierra Nevada glistening with snow that was somehow somber as the jewelry of the dead. I took a nap and wept for no reason. We went to a magnificent flamenco concert on a hill across from the Alhambra and ate very late in the evening. I became quite ill. My friend had to leave for her home in Collioure. I spent the day reading my empty journal, the white pages swarming with nothing. At 5 a.m. I went to an airport hours away in the darkness, flew to Madrid, then from Madrid to Chicago sitting next to a girl of surpassing beauty who said that she was an Erasmus scholar, an honor of sorts. I slept for eight hours and dreamt that Erasmus was a girl. At a Chicago airport hotel I thought I was slipping away and was taken to a hospital in an ambulance and my journal was crushed in my pocket. I stayed in ER for seven hours and a Chinese magician restored me. At dawn I flew to Montana and barely recognized our dog. My advice is, do not try to inhabit another's soul. You have your own.

, , ,

The truest night of the hunter
is when like his prey
he never wakes up.

We were born short boys in tall grass.
We became the magicians who actually
sawed the girl in half. We were prosecuted
unfairly by the gods for this simple mistake
and exiled to the tropics where we wore
the masques of howler monkeys
until we became howler monkeys
in the fabulous zoo of our culture.
Now as an amateur surgeon I'm putting
the girl back together stitch by painful stitch
beside the creek in the winter twilight.
She begs me to stop. She wants to become
a night-blooming cereus only seen
every decade or so in the random dark.

, , ,

Only one cloud
is moving the wrong way
across the sky
on Sunday morning.

MUSE II

Pretty girls most often have pretty
parents but then for unknown genetic
reasons a beautiful woman is born
of homely parents. She is not happy
about being set aside by the gods.
At family gatherings truly ugly relatives
want to murder her but this is rarely
done in poetry since William Shakespeare.
Out in the orchard she is buggered
nearly to death by her cousins who all
become scientists who devise products
we never imagined we would need.
She is sent into the world. She crawls
into the low door of the city but yearns
to stand straight. She floats up a river
into the country and lives with wild dogs
who are soon hunted to death for sport.
She wants to step off the world but can't find
the edge. A man flies her to Mexico
and makes her a prostitute. She escapes
but a pimp slashes her face, a happy
moment because now she's not beautiful.
She walks twenty miles down an empty beach
and lives with an old, deaf fisherman.
Now her soul swells with the grandeur of the ocean,
the beauty of fish, the silence of man,
the moon and stars she finally understands.

, , ,

The girl kissed a girl,
the boy kissed a boy.
What would become of them?

POET AT NINETEEN IN NYC

The poet looking for an immortal poem
from his usual pathetic position as a graduate
student in a university that doesn't exist.
He knows three constellations, this expert
of the stars, and sometimes notices the moon
by the time it reaches its first quarter.
He's admirable and keeps his chin high
in the city's arctic winds. He drinks
a hundred drinks a month, three a day
and a bit more for courage. He has a room
and a half, the half a tiny kitchenette,
and his table for writing and eating
is a piece of plywood he places on the bed.
Tacked above the bed are pictures of his heroes,
Dostoyevsky, Whitman, Lorca and Faulkner,
and of course Rimbaud. He doesn't fear rejection
because he keeps his work to himself. He thinks
he's as inevitable as a river but doesn't have time
to keep time. The hardest part is when the river
is too swift and goes underground for days on end.

, , ,

The violent wind.
The violent wind.
The violent wind.

SISTER

I wanted to play a song for you
on our old $28 phonograph
from 1954 but the needle is missing
and they no longer make the needles.
It is the work of man to make a voice
a needle. You were buried at nineteen
in wood with Daddy. I've spent a lifetime
trying to learn the language of the dead.
The musical chatter of the tiny yellow finches
in the front yard comes closest. It's midnight
and I'm giving my nightly rub to the dog's
tummy, something she truly depends on.
Maybe you drifted upward as an ancient
bird hoping to nest on the moon.

′ ′ ′

On watch on the ship's stern.
The past disappears
with the ship's wake
and the furling dark waters.

SKULL

You can't write the clear biography
of the aches and pains inside your skull.
Will I outlive my passport expiration?
Will the knots of the past beat me to death
like limber clubs, the Gordian knots
that never will be untied, big as bowling balls?
Maybe not. Each time I row the river
for six hours or so the innards of my skull
slightly change shape. Left alone knots
can unravel in the turbulence of water.
It isn't for me to understand why loved ones
died. My skull can't withstand
the Tao of the mighty river carrying me along
as if I were still and the mountains
capped by clouds were rushing past.
After we submerge do we rise again in another form?
Meanwhile I speculate on the seven pills
I must take each day to stay alive.
I ask each one, "Are we doing your job?"
The only answer I've found is the moving
water whose music is without a single lyric.

...

A local girl walked over the top
of the Absaroka Mountain Range
and was never seen again. Some say
a grizzly bear got her, some say aliens,
I think that fueled by loneliness
she is still walking.

HORSES

In truth I am puzzled most in life
by nine horses.

I've been watching them for eleven weeks
in a pasture near Melrose.

Two are on one side of the fence and seven
on the other side.

They stare at one another from the same places
hours and hours each day.

This is another unanswerable question
to haunt us with the ordinary.

They have to be talking to one another
in a language without a voice.

Maybe they are speaking the wordless talk of lovers,
sullen, melancholy, jubilant.

Linguists say that language comes after music
and we sang nonsense syllables

before we invented a rational speech
to order our days.

’ ’ ’

One day a heron walked
up our front steps and looked
into the front-door window.
Was it a heron and also
something else?

We live far out in the country where I hear
creature voices night and day.

Like us they are talking about their lives
on this brief visit to earth.

In truth each day is a universe in which
we are tangled in the light of stars.

Stop a moment. Think about these horses
in their sweet-smelling silence.

, , ,

Years ago at the cabin when returning
from the saloon at night
I'd scratch the ears of a bear
who'd rest his chin on the car windowsill.

What are these legitimate fruits
of daring?
The natural brain, bruised by mental
somersaults.
On a bet to sleep naked
out in the snow.
To push your forefingers into your ears
until they meet the brain.
To climb backwards into the heavens because
we poets live in reverse.
It is too late to seduce the heroine
in my stories.
How can enough be enough
when it isn't?
The Great Mother has no ears and *hallelujah*
is the most impossible word in the language.
I can only say it to birds, fish, and dogs.

＇ ＞ ＞

Azure. All told a year of water.
Some places with no bottom.
I had hoped to understand it
but it wasn't possible. Fish.

XMAS CHEESEBURGERS

I was without Christmas spirit
so I made three cow dogs,
Lola and Blacky and Pinto,
cheeseburgers with ground chuck
and French St. André cheese
so that we'd all feel better.
I delivered them to Hard Luck Ranch
and said, "Chew each bite 32 times."
They ignored me and gobbled.
The world that used to nurse us
now keeps shouting inane instructions.
That's why I ran to the woods.

, , ,

She told me in white tennis shorts
that when you think you can't
take it anymore you're just getting started.
No pieces can be put back together.

Mary, spayed early so a virgin like her ancient namesake, is a drug addict. She was stomped on as a puppy by an angry little girl and thus a lifetime of spinal problems. Now an old woman she waits for her pain pills every day and then she's a merry animal. Up until a few years back she'd run much farther than her Lab sister until she was a tiny black peppercorn in the alfalfa field. She walks much closer now turning to check if I'm following along. She's an English cocker and sniffs the ground then pauses to meditate on the scent. To understand Mary we have to descend into the cellar, the foundation of our being, the animal bodies we largely ignore. She sleeps a lot, eats kibble without interest and craves meat tidbits with the pleasure making her wiggle. Outdoors, her eyes wide to the open she acts with exuberance, our lost birthright. Like all beautiful women she has become beautifully homely. In the evening I lift her onto the couch despite her brush with a skunk, and we speak a bone-deep language without nouns and verbs, a creature-language skin to skin.

, , ,

Last week in this pasture it was 75.
Today it's 29 and snowing. The world is too small
with a limited amount of weather
with no cosmic 15,000-mph winds.
A piece of luck!

NIGHT CREATURES

"The horses run around, their feet
are on the ground." In my headlights
there are nine running down the highway,
clack-clacking in the night, swerving
and drifting, some floating down the ditch,
two grays, the rest colorless in the dark.
What can I do for them? Nothing, night
is swallowing all of us, the fences
on each side have us trapped,
the fences tight to the ditches. Suddenly they turn.
I stop. They come back toward me,
my window open to the glorious smell of horses.
I'm asking the gods to see them home.

’ ’ ’

These birds. Cutting up often dreary
life and letting joy seep through.
What are they? It's not for me to know
but to sense, to feel flight and song,
even in today's gray snowy sky.

A bit flinty. Trace of a squeak.
Does she hear herself?
"I hear only my own music," said Beethoven.
Is it an announcement or warning
from one so small and crippled
in youth by a child
who stomped her spine?
She listens to the glory of her past.
She knows where she is
in our home. She's Mary,
the deer chaser, a woman
of power, a lion in her mind,
roaring so weakly into the dark,
trying to make hips follow chest.

, , ,

Why does the mind compose this music
well before the words occur? The gods
created the sun and we the lightbulb
and the medicine that kept the happy child alive.

JUNE THE HORSE

Sleep is water. I'm an old man surging
upriver on the back of my dream horse
that I haven't seen since I was ten.
We're night riders through cities, forests, fields.

I saw Stephanie standing on the steps of Pandora's Box
on Sheridan Square in 1957. She'd never spoken
to me but this time, as a horse lover, she waved.

I saw the sow bear and two cubs. She growled
at me in 1987 when I tried to leave the cabin while her cubs
were playing with my garbage cans. I needed a drink
but I didn't need this big girl on my ass.

We swam up the Neva in St. Petersburg in 1972
where a girl sat on the bank hugging a red icon
and Raskolnikov, pissed off and whining, spat on her feet.

On the Rhône in the Camargue fighting bulls
bellowed at us from a marsh and 10,000 flamingos
took flight for Africa.

This night-riding is the finest thing I do at age seventy-two.
On my birthday evening we'll return to the original
pasture where we met and where she emerged from the pond
draped in lily pads and a coat of green algae.
We were children together and I never expected her return.

, , ,

Some of my friends sought their deathbeds,
Celtic dogs with their death tails
in their teeth. I thought I knew
them but I didn't. They ignored birds.

One day as a brown boy I shot a wasp nest with bow and arrow,
releasing hell. I mounted her from a stump and without
reins or saddle we rode to a clear lake where the bottom
was covered with my dreams waiting to be born.
One day I'll ride her as a bone-clacking skeleton.
We'll ride to Veracruz and Barcelona, then up to Venus.

＇ ＇ ＇

Late October and now I wear a wool
cap around the clock, take three naps a day.
I've no clear memory why this happens,
something about the earth tilting on an axis.
Yesterday twenty-three sandhill cranes flew north. Why?

POET NO. 7

We must be bareback riders. The gods
abhor halters and stirrups, even a horse
blanket to protect our asses is forbidden.
Finally, our legs must grow into the horse
because we were never meant to get off.

, , ,

I pray for seven women I know
who have cancer. I can't tell you why
they have cancer and neither can doctors.
They are beaten by a stranger with no face.

A PUZZLE

I see today that everyone on earth
wants the answer to the same question
but none has the language to ask it.
The inconceivable is clearly the inconceivable.
Bum mutter, teethchatter, brain flotsam,
we float up from our own depths
to the sky not the heavens, an invention
of the murderers. Dogs know the answer
by never asking the question but can't advise us.
Here is the brain that outran the finish line:
on a dark day when the world was slate
the yellow sun blasted the mountain across
the river so that it flung its granitic light
in the four directions to which we must bow.
Life doesn't strangle on ironies, we made
that part up. Close after dawn the sheep next door
leave their compound, returning at twilight.
With the rains this was a prodigious green year,
and now the decay of autumn sleeps in dead comfort.
Words are moving water — muddy, clear, or both.

, , ,

Recently ghosts are more solid than we are,
they have color and meat on their bones,
even odor and voices. You can only tell them
by what's missing. A nose, ear, feet on backward,
their hair that floats though the air is still.

RUMINATION

I sit up late dumb as a cow,
which is to say
somewhat conscious with thirst
and hunger, an eye for the new moon
and the morning's long walk
to the water tank. Everywhere
around me the birds are waiting
for the light. In this world of dreams
don't let the clock cut up
your life in pieces.

, , ,

We fear the small hole in our brain
that made its tubular descent to the center of the earth
when we were born. In the loveliest landscape,
the tinge of death. The photo of the mammoth grizzly
gaining on the young buffalo? No, the tinge is in the air.

DAN'S BUGS

I felt a little bad about the nasty earwig
that drowned in my nighttime glass of water,
lying prone at the bottom like a shipwrecked mariner.
There was guilt about the moth who died
when she showered with me, possibly a female.
They communicate through wing vibrations.
I was careful when sticking a letter
in our rural mailbox, waiting for a fly to escape,
not wanting her to be trapped there in the darkness.
Out here in the country many insects invade our lives
and many die in my nightcap, floating and deranged.
On the way to town to buy wine and a chicken
I stopped from 70 mph to pick up
a wounded dragonfly fluttering on the yellow line.
I've read that some insects live only for minutes,
as we do in our implacable geologic time.

, , ,

Fifty years ago in our cold, snowbound
house in the north, Carlos Montoya brought sunlight.
When I finally went to Seville and Granada,
the cold house sometimes entered my hotel rooms,
a flash of snowdrifts among the orange trees.

INVISIBLE

Within the wilder shores of sky
billions of insects are migrating
for reasons of sex and food,
or so I'm told by science,
in itself as invisible as the specters
of love and death. What can I see
from here but paper and the mind's
random images? A living termite
was found on sticky paper at 19,000 feet.
Perhaps she thought she had lost
the world as I think I must, barring
flora, fauna, family, dogs, the earth,
the mind ground of being as it is.
A few years back I began to lose
the world of people. I couldn't hold on.
Rüppell's vulture was seen at 36,000 feet
for reasons the gods keep from us.

, , ,

Off Ecuador the whale was so close I could smell
her oily smell, look into a soccer-ball eye.
I was frightened when the motor quit
and I couldn't see land. Now I can't see
the ocean in the mountains, only watch the rivers run.

MARY

How can this dog on the cushion
at my feet have passed me
in the continuum of age, a knot
in our hearts that never unwinds? This dog
is helplessly herself and cannot think otherwise.
When called she often conceals herself
behind a bush, a tree, or tall grass
pondering if she should obey. Now crippled
at twelve, bearing up under pain
on the morning run, perhaps wondering
remotely what this is all about, the slowness
that has invaded her bones. Splayed out
now in a prone running pose
she moves in sleep slowly into the future
that does not welcome us but is merely
our destiny in which we disappear
making room for others on the long march.
The question still is how did she pass me
happily ahead in this slow goodbye?

﹐ ﹐ ﹐

After a long siege of work
I wake up to a different world.
I'm older of course, but colors and shapes
have changed. The mountains have moved a bit,
our children are older. How could this happen?

Yes, in the predawn black
the slim slip of the waning moon,
the cuticle of an unknown god,
perhaps Mother Night, the outline
of her back between points of stars,
she's heading south toward Mexico
preferring mountains, rivers, oceans, jungles
that return her affection for earth.
It's been hard work to guide migrating
birds for 150 million years. To her
we're newcomers, but then she married
me, a stranger whom she's worn thin as water.

′ ′ ′

When young I read that during the Philippine War
we shot six hundred Indians in a wide pit. It didn't seem fair.
During my entire life I've been helpless
in this matter. I even dream about it.

In my recent studies I have discovered cancer.
Last year it was the language of birds
and the year before, time by drowning a clock in the toilet.
It is life's work to recognize the mystery
of the obvious. Cancer is a way the gods
have learned to kill us. In numbers it's tied
with war and famine. Time is the way
our deaths are numbered precisely. The birds
and their omnipresent language, their music,
have resisted conclusions as surely as the stars
above them which they use for navigation.
I have prayed willingly to their disinterest,
the way they look past me into the present,
their songs greeting both daylight and dark.
They've been on earth fifty times longer than us
right down to the minute, and they've told me
that cancer and time are only death's music,
that we learned this music before birth without hearing it.
Like cancer cells we've lost our way and will do anything to live.
My mind can't stop its only child so frightened of the dark.

’ ’ ’

I read so much that my single eye became hot
as if it had been staring into nebulae.
Of course it had. On some clear nights in the country
the stars can exhaust us. They only mean what they are.

ACHE

All this impermanence and suffering
we share with dogs, bees, crows,
the aquatic insect that lives but a single
minute on a summer evening
then descends to its river burial,
perhaps into the mouth of a trout
already full of its brothers and sisters
while in a nearby meadow the she
wolf approaches an infant elk
she'll share with her litter.
Many of us live full term never seeing
the bullet, the empty plate of hunger,
the invisible noose of disease.
We can't imagine the rings of the bristlecone
that lived for millennia. We cut it down
to number the years like our own insolent birthdays.

, , ,

In summer I walk the dogs at dawn
before the rattlesnakes awake. In cold weather
I walk the dogs at dawn out of habit.
In the pastures we find many oval deer beds
of crushed grass. Their bodies are their homes.

ORIOLE

Emerging after three months to the edge
of the hole of pain I arrange
ten orange halves on a stiff wire
off the patio between a small tree
and the feeder. Early next morning
five orioles of three species appear:
Scott's, hooded, Bullock's. Thinking
of those long nights: this is what agony wanted,
these wildly colored birds to inhabit
my mind far from pain.
Now they live inside me.

, , ,

The tree only intends what it is with its dictator
genome. Like us they don't see what's coming.
They often rot from inside out though it can take
decades. When sawed down you smell the sharp
edged ripeness of their lives, their blood.

BLUE SHAWL

The other day at the green dumpsters,
an old woman in a blue shawl
told me that she loved my work.

, , ,

The clouds are only a foot above my head
and there's a brisk cold wind from the north.
Still, when I pass the yard headed for the hills
the garden is lavish with dying and dead
flowers, so many wild immutable colors
that my cold head soars up through the clouds.

RIVER I

I was there in a room in a village
by the river when the moon fell into the window
frame and was trapped there too long.
I was fearful but I was upside down
and my prayers fell off the ceiling.
Our small dog Jacques jumped on the sofa
near the window, perched on the sofa's back
and released the moon to head south.
Just after dawn standing in the green yard
I watched a girl ride down the far side
of the railroad tracks on a beauteous white horse
whose lower legs were wrapped in red tape.
Above her head were mountains covered with snow.
I decided we were born to be moving water not ice.

﹐ ﹐ ﹐

Out in the pasture I found the second concealed
hole descending to a room sculpted from hard dirt.
The previous owner was frightened of atomic attack.
Now it's the home of the beast god forgot to invent.
This is where our bodies will sit down to eat us.

RIVER II

Another dawn in the village by the river
and I'm jealous of the 63 moons of Jupiter.
Out in the yard inspecting a lush lilac bush
followed by five dogs who have chosen
me as their temporary leader. I look up
through the vodka jangle of the night before,
straight up at least 30,000 feet where the mountains
are tipping over on me. Dizzy I grab the lilacs
for support. Of course it's the deceitful clouds
playing the game of becoming mountains.
Once on our nighttime farm on a moonlit walk
the clouds pushed by a big western wind
became a school of whales swimming hard
across the cold heavens and I finally knew
that we walk the bottom of an ocean we call sky.

, , ,

On television I saw a tall willowy girl jump
seven feet in the air. How grand to have a dozen
of these girls weaving in and out of the pines
and willows in the yard and jumping so high,
perhaps to Stravinsky, the landscape visible
under their bodies. They don't have to be nice.
Art often isn't though it scrubs the soul fresh.
The beauty of the rattlesnake is in its threat.

RIVER III

Saw a poem float by just beneath
the surface, another corpse of the spirit
we weren't available to retrieve.
It isn't comforting to admit that our days
are fatal, that the corpse of the spirit
gradually becomes the water and waits
for another, or perhaps you, to return
to where you belong, not in the acting
of a shaker sprinkling its salt
everywhere. You have to hold your old
heart lightly as the female river holds
the clouds and trees, its fish
and the moon, so lightly but firmly
enough so that nothing gets away.

, , ,

As the Bulgarians say, the moon is to blame.
Come to think of it that's right. The moon
works in waves of power like the ocean
and I was swept away into wrongdoing
when the moon was large. I am innocent.

The river seems confused today because it
swallowed the thunderstorm above us. At my age
death stalks me but I don't mind. This is to be
expected but how can I deal with the unpardonable
crime of loneliness? The girl I taught to swim
so long ago has gone to heaven, the kind of thing
that happens while we're on the river fishing and
seeing the gorgeously colored western tanagers and the
profusion of nighthawks that some call bullbats,
nightjars, and down on the border they call them
goatsuckers for stealing precious milk. I love
this misfiring of neurons in which I properly
understand nothing, not the wild high current
or the thunderstorm on which it chokes. Did the
girl swim to heaven through the ocean of sky?
Maybe. I can deny nothing. Two friends are mortally
ill. Were it not for the new moon my sky
would collapse tonight so fed by the waters of memory.

’ ’ ’

Of late I can wake up and the world
isn't quite recognizable or I'm finally
with age losing my touch, my control.
Three days seemed identical but then they were
and perhaps in losing my self all became lucid.
This isn't a brave new world but one finally revealed.

RIVER V

Resting in an eddy against dense greenery
so thick you can't see into it but can fathom
its depth by waning birdcalls, hum of insects.
This morning I learned that we live and die
as children to the core only carrying
as a protective shell a fleshy costume
made up mostly of old scar tissue
from before we learned how to protect ourselves.
It's hard to imagine that this powerful
river had to begin with a single drop
far into the mountains, a seep or trickle
from rocks and then the runoff from snowmelt.
Of course watershed means the shedding
of water, rain, a hundred creeks, a thousand
small springs. My mind can't quite
contain this any more than my own inception
in a single sperm joining a single egg
utterly invisible, hidden in Mother's moist
dark. Out of almost nothing, for practical
purposes nothing, then back as ancient
children to the great nothing again,
the song of man and water moving to the ocean.

, , ,

The brush I scrub my soul with each morning
is made of the ear-hairs of a number of animals:
dogs, pigs, deer, goat, raccoon, a wolverine,
and pinfeathers of particular birds, a secret.
Brush too hard, your ambitions will be punished.

RIVER VI

I thought years ago that old Heraclitus was wrong.
You can't step into the same river even once.
The water slips around your foot like liquid time
and you can't dry it off after its passage.
Don't bother taking your watch to the river,
the moving water is a glorious second hand.
Properly understood the memory loses nothing
and we humans are never allowed to let our minds
sit on the still bank and have a simple picnic.
I had an unimaginable dream when young
of being a river horse that could easily plunge upstream.
Perhaps it came from our huge black mare June
whom I rode bareback as she swam the lake
in big circles, always getting out where she got in.
Meanwhile this river is surrounded by mountains
covered with lodgepole pines that are mortally diseased,
browning in the summer sun. Everyone knows
that lightning will strike and Montana burn.
We all stay quiet about it, this blessed oxygen
that makes the world a crematory. Only the water is safe.

’ ’ ’

I took the girl to the dance but she returned
with another. I forgave her. I took her to another
dance and she went home with two men. I forgave
her again. This became a pattern, I forgave
her so the maggots of hatred wouldn't eat my brain.

RIVER VII

The last trip to the river this year. Tonight I think
of the trout swimming in a perfect, moonless
dark, navigating in the current by the tiny pinpoint
of stars, night wind rippling the eddies,
and always if you stick your head under
the surface, the slight sound of the pebbles
rubbing against pebbles. Today I saw two dead
pelicans. I heard they are shot because they eat
trout, crows shot because they eat duck eggs,
wolves shot for eating elk or for chasing
a bicyclist in Yellowstone. Should we be shot
for eating the world and giving back our puke?
Way down in Notch Bottom, ancient winter camp
for long-gone Indians, I am sweetly consoled
by our absolute absence except for a stretch
of fence on the bank, half washed away
by the current, a sequence of No Trespassing signs
to warn us away from a pricey though miasmic swamp.
The river can't heal everything. You have to do your part.
We've even bruised the moon. Still the birds are a chorus
with the moving flow, clearly relatives of Mozart,
the brown trout so lovely the heart flutters. Back home
something has eaten the unfledged swallows. It wasn't us.
I'm on another river now, it's swollen and turbulent.
"The spirit is here. Are you?" I ask myself.

, , ,

The night is long for a hungry dog.
We're not with them in spirit. They're alone.
The small teddy bear Lulu gave me in France
suddenly tipped over on my desk. Does this mean
my beloved is dead? She's ninety-three. Her
food and wine were the essence of earth.

Something new in the air today, perhaps the struggle of the bud to become a leaf. Nearly two weeks late it invaded the air but then what is two weeks to life herself? On a cool night there is a break from the struggle of becoming. I suppose that's why we sleep. In a childhood story they spoke of "the land of enchantment." We crawl to it, we short-lived mammals, not realizing that we are already there. To the gods the moon is the entire moon but to us it changes second by second because we are always fish in the belly of the whale of earth. We are encased and can't stray from the house of our bodies. I could say that we are released, but I don't know, in our private night when our souls explode into a billion fragments then calmly regather in a black pool in the forest, far from the cage of flesh, the unremitting "I." This was a dream and in dreams we are forever alone walking the ghost road beyond our lives. Of late I see waking as another chance at spring.

, , ,

In the Upper Peninsula of Michigan
and mountains of the Mexican border
I've followed the calls of birds
that don't exist into thickets
and up canyons. I'm unsure
if all of me returned.

SKY

Here along the Mexican border
working on the patio between
two bamboo thickets and facing
the creek, all that I hear while
staring down at the unforgiving paper
is chatter and song,
the crisp fluff of birds flying
back and forth to the feeders,
the creek that actually burbles,
and the nearly imperceptible sound
of the sky straining to keep
us on earth despite our disappointments,
our fatal cries that disappear
into her blueness, her blackness.

, , ,

I left this mangy little
three-legged bear two big fish
on a stump. He ate them at night
and at dawn slept like a god
leaning against the stump
in a chorus of birds.

MARCH IN PATAGONIA, AZ

Some days in March are dark
and some altogether too glittery
and loud with birds. There is recent news
of ancient cosmic events that have lost
significance. I recognize the current
moon from Granada several years
ago, a big Spanish moon though here
it hangs over Mexico, shining on blood
and the music wandering lost in the air.
At the ranch starving cattle
bawl loudly in the drought.

, , ,

The day was so dulcet and beautiful
I could think about nothing.
I lost my head.

BRAZIL

"It rains most in the ocean off Trinidad
so that the invisible sea flowers
never stop blooming on the lid of water."

Or so she said on a balcony in Bahia
in 1982, brushing her long black hair
upward into the wet moonlit night.

I'm staring east at the island of Itaparica
spangled with light a dozen miles at sea.
I think that it's not for me to determine the truth.

A half hour ago it was a snake far to the west
in the jungle which only ate flowers the color
of blood and laid seven red eggs every year.

In Brazil I'm adding to my knowledge
of the impossible. In her remote hometown
a condor stole and raised a child as its own.

At dinner of a roasted fish she said the child
had learned to fly and I broke, saying no,
that our arms have the wrong kind of feathers.

She was pissed and said, "I went to Miami
with an aunt when I was seven to fix my heart.
You only make guns, bombs, cars, and count money.

, , ,

A big warm wind in November,
yellow willow leaves
swirl around one hundred
white sheep.
This world is going to sleep.

"Your ocean stank of gasoline, your food was white.
I saw an alligator eat a dog. A river
didn't run into the sea but went backwards.

"A century ago in my hometown the Virgin Mary
appeared and sang about her lost child in the river
of men. If you don't believe me you're wicked."

Back home in the cold our dogs run across
clear ice, their feet and shadows watched by fish.
I drop three lighted candles into moving water to survive Brazil.

’ ’ ’

Woke up from a nap and in an instant
knew I was alive. It was startling
to the point of fear. Emotions and sensations
were drowning me. This had never happened before.
On a blue chair in a pasture I relearned the world.

GRAND MARAIS

The wind came up so strongly at midnight
the cabin creaked in its joints and between
the logs, the tin roof hummed and shuddered
and in the woods you could hear the dead
trees called widow-makers falling
with staccato crashes, and by 3 a.m.
the thunderous roar of Lake Superior miles away.
My dog Rose comes from the sofa
where she invariably sleeps. Her face is close
to mine in the dark, a question on her breath.
Will the sun rise again? She gets on the bed trembling.
I wonder what the creature life is doing
without shelter? Rose is terribly frightened
of this lordly old bear I know who visits
the yard for the sunflower seeds I put out
for the birds. I placed my hand on his head one night
through the car window when I was drunk.
He doesn't give a shit about violent storms
knowing the light comes from his mind, not the sun.

,   ,   ,

I've heard it three times from the woods,
le cri de Merlin. Fear is the price
you pay for remoteness, pure fear, somber
and penetrating. Maybe it's just that female wolf
I saw. The world is not what we thought it was.

DESERT SNOW

I don't know what happens after death
but I'll have to chance it. I've been waking
at 5 a.m. and making a full study of darkness.
I was upset not hearing the predicted rain
that I very much need for my wildflowers.
At first light I see that it was the silent rain
of snow. I didn't hear this softest sigh
of windless snow softly falling
here on the Mexican border in the mountains,
snow in a white landscape of high desert.
The birds are confounded by this rare snow
so I go out with a spatula to clean the feeders,
turn on the radio not to the world's wretched news
but to the hot, primary colors of cantina music,
the warbles and shrieks of love, laughter, and bullets.

, , ,

In the Yucatán the jungle was from the movies
until the second day, then became itself.
I go away then come home but the jungle's
birds and snakes are with me in the snow.
You carry with you all the places you've ever been.

REALITY

Nothing to console the morning but the dried grasshopper
on my desk who fell apart at my powerful touch.
Two days ago at dawn I awoke with a large black tear
stuck to my cheek that felt like a globule of tar.
The MRI machine at the Nogales hospital revealed
that the black tear is connected to heart, brain, penis
with three pieces of nearly invisible spiderweb.
My friend the urologist said that if even one breaks
Eros is dead in my body, a corpse of the memory of love.
Luckily I was diverted for a day by helping my wife
make Thanksgiving dinner for ten friends and neighbors,
brooding about the souls of 35 million turkeys
hovering visibly in the blue sky above our naked earth.
They can't fly away like the game birds I hunt, doves and quail.
As with people we've bred them so that they're unable to escape.
At certain remote locations they see through the fence
their mysterious cousins flying to tree limbs
and weep dry turkey tears of bitter envy.
I made the gravy, the most important substance on earth,
but now on Friday morning I'm back to my black tear
on my old brown cheek of barely alive Eros.
In slightly more than a week I'll be seventy-two.
How can I concoct this intricate fantasy of making love
to three French girls on a single Paris afternoon?
It begins with a not very good pot of coffee
in my room at the Hôtel de Suède on rue Vaneau
where at night I heard an owl, a chouette in the garden.

＇＇＇

In a foreign city, even New York, I'm never
convinced I'll get back home where I wish to be.
It seems unlikely. The routes disappear.
You can follow the birds home but they're too fast
and often change their minds. Especially crows.

I meet two of the girls in the Luxembourg on a morning walk
where one, astoundingly, is reading a novel I wrote.
I demand ID to make sure they're of legal age.
One must be safe from the police in fantasies.
We go shopping and I buy them 100-euro
tricornered hats. We go to an apartment
and meet the older sister of one. She's twenty-three.
I sign my books they own and when I turn
they sit on the sofa with soft cotton skirts raised.
I forgot to add that it's a warm day in April.
Should I choose by saying, "Eeny, meeny, miney, mo,"
or would this Michigan idiom frighten them?
I make a dream swan dive into a day of love and laughter
then suddenly I'm back at Hard Luck Ranch
giving the cow dogs biscuits. Old nitwit Petey
pisses in his food and water as Man in Our Time.
I am liberated back into the fragility of childhood.

, , ,

Reading Gilfillan's *Warbler Road* I learn
what I don't care about anymore by its absence.
These tiny birds are the living jewelry of the gods.
They clothe my life in proper mystery telling me
that all is not lost, harboring as they do stillborn children.

Nothing is as it appears to be.
What is this aging? What am I to make
of these pale, brutal numbers? For a moment I'm fourteen.
The sky didn't fall in, it fell out.
Men suck on their sugary black pistols
but the world isn't ruled for a second.
The pen is mightier than the sword
only in the fretwork of a poet's language.
At fourteen green was green and women
were the unreachable birds of night,
their fronts and backs telling us
we might not be alone in the universe,
their voices singing that the earth is female.
The humid summer night was as warm as birth,
and she swam out into the night beyond the dock light.

′ ′ ′

I'm quite tired of beating myself up
to write. I think I'll start letting
the words slip out like a tired child.
"Can I have a piece of pie" he asks,
and then he's asleep back on the cusp of the moon.

LOVE

Love is raw as freshly cut meat,
mean as a beetle on the track of dung.
It is the Celtic dog that ate its tail in a dream.
It chooses us as a blizzard chooses a mountain.
It's seven knocks on the door you pray not to answer.
The boy followed the girl to school eating his heart
with each step. He wished to dance with her
beside a lake, the wind showing the leaves'
silvery undersides. She held the moist bouquet
of wild violets he had picked against her neck.
She wore the sun like her skin
but beneath, her blood was black as soil.
At the grave of her dog in the woods
she told him to please go away forever.

＇ ＇ ＇

Again I wonder if I'll return.
France twice this fall, then New York. Will I know
if I don't return? The basic question of life.
Does Robert Frost know he's dead? His Yankee wit
a dust mote. God's stories last until no one hears.

The tears roll up my cheek
and the car backs itself south.
I pull away from the girl and reverse
through the door without looking.
In defiance of the body the mind
does as it wishes, the crushed bones
of life reknit themselves in sunlight.
In the night the body melts itself
down to the void before birth
before you swam the river into being.
Death takes care of itself like a lightning
stroke and the following thunder
is the veil being rent in twain.
The will to live can pass away
like that raven colliding with the sun.
In age we tilt toward home.
We want to sleep a long time, not forever,
but then to sleep a long time becomes forever.

, , ,

The fly on the window is not a distant crow
in the sky. We're forced into these decisions.
People are forever marrying the wrong people
and the children of the world suffer.
Their dreams hang in the skies out of reach.

They used to say we're living on borrowed
time but even when young I wondered
who loaned it to us? In 1948 one grandpa
died stretched tight in a misty oxygen tent,
his four sons gathered, his papery hand
grasping mine. Only a week before, we were fishing.
Now the four sons have all run out of borrowed time
while I'm alive wondering whom I owe
for this indisputable gift of existence.
Of course time is running out. It always
has been a creek heading east, the freight
of water with its surprising heaviness
following the slant of the land, its destiny.
What is lovelier than a creek or riverine thicket?
Say it is an unknown benefactor who gave us
birds and Mozart, the mystery of trees and water
and all living things borrowing time.
Would I still love the creek if I lasted forever?

, , ,

There's no question about circles, curves,
and loops, life's true structures, but the edges,
straight lines, squares come from us.
We must flee these shapes, even linear sentences
that limit us to doors, up and down ladders,
straight trajectories which will curve in eternity.

PRISONERS

In truth I have lost my beauty
but this isn't as important as the violation
of the myth of the last meal due those
about to be executed. I believe in the sacred
obligation to give a man about to be dead
what he wants to eat. Not true. In Texas
it's limited to what's on hand, the hundreds
of tons of frozen garbage prisoners feed on.
Not to worry. I'm ineligible to be executed,
not being convicted of killing anyone, but after
a lifetime of chewing I'd choose a saltine cracker.
After all, we chew and chew and chew. Pigs, fish,
melancholy cows and gamboling lambs pass
through us, not to speak of fields of wheat
and lettuce, tomatoes and beans. Our jaws are strong
as a woman's thighs pumping up the stairs
of a tall building to throw herself from the roof
because she's tired of chewing, being penetrated
by swallowing, and of a man who chews
as if his life depended on it, which it does.

, , ,

In Africa back in 1972 one day I studied
a female lion with blood on her fluttering whiskers,
traces of dark blood on her muzzle. A creature died
as we all must. In my seventies I see the invisible
lion not stalking but simply waiting, the solution
of the mystery I don't want to solve. She's waiting.

CORRUPTION

Like Afghanistan I'm full of corruption.
My friend McGuane once said, "I'd gladly
commit a hundred acts of literary capitulation
to keep my dog in Alpo." The little ones needed
dental braces and flutes, cars and houses.
Off and on I've had this dangerous golden touch
like a key to a slot machine streaming 20-dollar
gold pieces. It was so easy to buy expensive
French wine that purges the grim melancholy
of livelihood, the drudgery of concocting fibs.
I know a man, happily married, who bought
a girl a hundred-dollar pair of panties. I was stunned.
For this price I buy a whole lamb each fall.
Now lamb and panties are gone though the panties
might be on a card table at a yard sale.
Right now a wind has come up and there's a strange
blizzard of willow buds outside my studio.
I'm on death row but won't give up corruption.
I've waterboarded myself. I'm guilty of everything.

＞　＞　＞

One day near here there was an earthquake
that started a new river in the mountains. During
the ponderous snowmelt in spring the river
is hundreds of feet deep and massive boulders roll
crashing along the bottom though you can't see them.

OUR ANNIVERSARY

I want to go back to that wretched old farm
on a cold November morning eating herring
on the oil tablecloth at daylight, the hard butter
in slivers and chunks on rye bread, gold-colored
homemade butter. Fill the woodbox, Jimmy.
Clots of cream in the coffee, hiss and crackle
of woodstove. Outside it's been the hardest freeze
yet but the heels still break through into the earth.
A winter farm is dead and you want to head for the woods.
In the barn the smell of manure and still-green hay
hit the nose with the milk in the metal pails.
Grandpa is on the last of seven cows,
tugging their dicklike udders, a squirt in the mouth
for the barn cat. My girlfriend loves another
and at twelve it's as if all the trees have died.
Sixty years later seven hummingbirds at the feeder,
miniature cows in their stanchions sipping liquid sugar.
We are fifty years together. There are still trees.

, , ,

I've traveled back to the invention of trees
but never water. Water is too far in the blind past
whereas trees have eyes that help us see
their penetration of earth. Much that you see
isn't with your eyes. Throughout the body are eyes.

DOORS

I'm trying to create an option for all
these doors in life. You're inside
or out, outside or in. Of late, doors
have failed us more than the two-party system
or marriages comprising only one person.
We've been fooled into thousands of dualisms
which the Buddha says is a bad idea.
Nature has portals rather than doors.
There are two vast cottonwoods near a creek
and when I walk between them I shiver.
Winding through my field of seventy-seven
large white pine stumps from about 1903
I take various paths depending on spirit.
The sky is a door never closed to us.
The sun and moon aren't doorknobs.
Dersu Uzala slept outside for forty-five years.
When he finally moved inside he died.

⸓ ⸓ ⸓

Of course we are condemned to life without parole
until the gods usher us in to our executioners
who live in a hot windowless room, always dark.
But then our fragility imagines everything
and the final moment is a kiss from the lipless gods.

GREED

I'm greedy for the pack rat to make
it across the swift creek. It's my first swimming
pack rat and I wonder why he wants the other side.
The scent of a pack-rat woman perhaps.
I'm greedy for those I prayed for to survive
cancer, greedy for money we don't need,
for the freshest fish to eat every day
without moving to the ocean's shore,
to have many lovers who don't ruin my marriage
and that my dog will live longer than me
to avoid the usual sharp boyhood heartbreak,
to regain the inch and a half I lost with age, to see
my youngest aunt pull up her nylons again in 1948.
Oh how I wanted a real sponge, a once-living
creature, and a wide chamois cloth to wash
cars for a quarter, a huge twenty-cent burger
and a five-cent Coca-Cola for lunch, greedy
that my beloved wife will last longer than me,
that the wind will blow harder up the girl's
summer dress, for three dozen oysters
and a bottle of 1985 Pétrus at twilight,
to smoke a cigarette again in a bar, that my
daughters live to be a hundred if they so wish,
that I march to heaven barefoot on a spring morning.

' ' '

Years before Hubble I thrust myself
far up into the night and saw that the constellations
were wildly colored. This frightened me
so I swam a river at night waiting for the stars
to resume their whiteness to adapt to my limits.

CEREAL

Late-night herring binge causes sour
gut. My dog ate the Hungarian partridge
eggs in the tall grass, her jaws dripping
yolk, therefore I ate a cereal for breakfast
guaranteed to restore my problematic health.
Soon enough I'll be diving for my own
herring in the North Atlantic, or running so fast
I nearly take off like the partridge mother
abandoning her eggs to the canine monster.
It will be strange to be physically magnificent
at my age, the crowds of girls cooing
around me as I bounce up and down
as if my legs cannot contain their pogo strength,
but I leave the girls behind, bouncing across
a river toward the end of the only map we have,
the not very wide map of the known world.

′ ′ ′

Where's my medicine bag? It's either hidden
or doesn't exist. Inside are memories of earth:
corn pollen, a bear claw, an umbilical cord.
If they exist they help me ride the dark
heavens of this life. Such fragile wings.

A winter dawn in New York City
with people rushing to work
eating rolls, drinking paper cups
of coffee. This isn't the march of the dead
but people moving toward their livelihoods
in this grim, cold first sign of daylight.
I watched the same thing in Paris
and felt like the eternal meddler sitting
at the window, trying to avoid
conclusions about humans, their need
to earn their daily bread, as we used to say.
In Paris I know a lovely woman
who wears a twenty-foot-long wool skirt
to hide her legs from men. Who can blame
her though I fear the grave dangers
of this trailing garment clipped and woven
from lowly sheep. What a burden
it is to drag this heavy skirt
throughout the workday to hide from desire
as if her sexuality had become a car bomb
rather than a secret housepet hidden
from the landlords of the world who are always there.

, , ,

In Fillmore, Utah, night of the full moon,
Nov. 20, a day of blizzard, driving rain,
at 4:44 a.m. I'm arranging my tiny petrified
truffles from the Dordogne on the motel table.
They look like the decayed teeth of a small predator.
I'll leave one behind to start a new civilization.

SUNLIGHT

After days of darkness I didn't understand
a second of yellow sunlight
here and gone through a hole in clouds
as quickly as a flashbulb, an immense
memory of a moment of grace withdrawn.
It is said that we are here but seconds in cosmic
time, twelve and a half billion years,
but who is saying this and why?
In the Salt Lake City airport eight out of ten
were fiddling relentlessly with cell phones.
The world is too grand to reshape with babble.
Outside the hot sun beat down on clumsy metal
birds and an actual ten-million-year-old
crow flew by squawking in bemusement.
We're doubtless as old as our mothers, thousands
of generations waiting for the sunlight.

＇ ＇ ＇

The birds of winter. How I brooded
about them in my childhood. Why not fly south?
In the kingdom of birds everyone lives until they don't.

BRUTISH

The man eating lamb's tongue salad
rarely thinks of the lamb.
The oral surgeon jerking twenty teeth out
in a day still makes marinara sauce.
The German sorting baby shoes at Treblinka
writes his wife and children frequently.
The woman loves her husband, drops two kids
at day care, makes passionate love
to an old boyfriend at the Best Western.
We are parts. What part are you now?
The shit of the world has to be taken
care of every day. You have to choose
your part after you take care of the shit.
I've chosen birds and fish, the creatures
whose logic I wish to learn and live.

, , ,

It's sudden. The chickadee hanging on a barb
of wire half eaten by the northern shrike. Birds kill
each other like we do but to eat. We're both five billion.
Whoever destroys their home rapes the gods.

NIGHTFEARS

What is it that you're afraid of at night?
Is it the gunman at the window, the rattler
slipping into your boot on the patio, the painful
quirk in your tummy or the semitruck
drifting across the centerline because the driver
is text-messaging a she-male girlfriend in El Paso?
Is it because so many birds these days are born
with one wing like poets in campus infirmaries,
that the ghouls of finance, or the post office,
have taken your paycheck to pay for Kool-Aid
parties around their empty pools? The night
has decided to stick around for a week
and people are confused, we creatures of habit
who took the sun for granted. She had decided
on whim to keep herself from us, calling down
the descent of a galactic cloud, to let flowers
wilt and die. Whole countries expire in hysteria
and troops must march in the glare of headlights.
When the red sun decides to rise again we humans
of earth swim through the acrid milk of our brains
toward the rising light, a new song on our lips,
but all creatures retreat from us, their murderers.
In real dawn's early light my poached egg is only an egg.

’ ’ ’

The body wins another little argument
with doom. You wake to a crisp, clear morning
and you're definitely not dead. The golden light
flows down the mountain across the creek. A little vodka
and twelve hours of sleep. Nature detonates your mind
with the incalculable freshness of the new day.

BLUE

During last night's blue moon
the Great Matter and Original Mind
were as close as your skin.
In the predawn dark you ate muskmelon
and the color of the taste lit up the mind.
The first finch awoke and the moon
descended into its mountain burial.

＞ ＞ ＞

The creek bed in front of our casita
has many tracks: javelina, deer, mountain
lion, and sometimes in the sand the serpentine
trace of a fat rattler. Foremost I love
the tracks left by hundreds of species of birds
that remain in the air like we do.

THE CURRENT POOR

The rich are giving the poor bright-colored
balloons, a dollar a gross, also bandages,
and leftover Mercurochrome from the fifties.
It is an autumn equinox and full moon present,
an event when night and day are precisely
equal, but then the poor know that night
always wins, grows wider and longer
until Christmas when they win a few minutes.
Under the tree there's an orange big as a basketball.
It is the exiled sun resting in its winter coolness.

, , ,

What vices we can hold in our Big Heads
and Big Minds, our Humor and Humility.
We don't march toward death, it marches toward us
as a summer thunderstorm came slowly across
the lake long ago. See the lightning of mortality dance,
the black clouds whirling as if a million crows.

MOPING

Please help me, gentle reader. I need advice.
I need to carbonate my brain
before nightfall. One more night
with this heaviness will suffocate me.
It's probably only the terror
of particulars. Memories follow us
like earaches in childhood. I'm surrounded
by sad-eyed burros, those motel paintings
I thought were book reviewers and politicians
but no, they're all my dead friends
who keep increasing in numbers until
it occurs to me that I might join them one day
floating out there in the anemic ether
of nothingness, but that's not my current business.
Just for the time being my brain needs oxygen
though I'm not sure what it is, life's puzzle
where you wake in a foreign land and the people
haven't shown themselves but the new birds
are haunting. The mind visits these alien Egypts,
these incalculable sunrises in a new place,
these birds of appetite with nowhere to land.

, , ,

Doom should be ashamed of itself.
It's so ordinary happening to billions
of creatures. It's common as a toilet seat,
the discarded shoes of a lifetime. It's proper
that it often hides itself until the last moment
and then the eternal silent music begins.

CHURCH

After last night's storm the tulip
petals are strewn across the patio
where they mortally fluttered. Only the gods
could reconnect them to their green stems
but they choose not to perform such banal
magic. Life bores deep holes in us
in hopes the nature of what we are
might sink into us without the blasphemy
of the prayer for parlor tricks. Ask the gods
to know them before you beg for favors.
The pack rat removes the petals one by one.
Now they are in a secret place, not swept away.
The death of flowers is unintentional. Who knows
if either of us will have a memory of ourselves?
If you stay up in the mountains it's always cold
but if you come down to the world of men you suffocate
in the folds of the overripe ass of piety, the smell
of alms not flowers, the smiling beast of greed.

, , ,

I'm unaware of what kind of singer I've become.
Each night there's a glass of vodka that quickly
becomes the color of my blood, the color of the guts
of archangels, the color pumped in dirt by the hearts
of soldiers. Any more than one glass of vodka
smears the constellations, the true source of light.

CHATTER

Back on the blue chair before the green studio
I'm keeping track of the outside world
rather than the inside where my brain seethes
in its usual mischief. Like many poets
I'm part blackbird and part red squirrel
and my brain chatters, shrieks, and whistles
but outside it tends to get real quiet
as if the greenery, garden, and mountains
can be put into half sleep though a female
blackbird is irritated with me. She's protecting
her fledgling child that died last Friday.
I placed a small white peony on its body.
Meanwhile the outside is full of the stuff of life.
Inside it's sitting there slumped with the burden
of memory and anecdotal knowledge, the birds of appetite
flitting here and there singing about sex and food,
the girl bending over with her impossible target,
or will it be foie gras or bologna and mayo?
The fish back then were larger and swam past
along with a few horses and dogs. Japanese
archers once used dogs for target practice
and that's why we won the war. A dead friend
still chatters his squirrel chatter like the squirrel
in the TV hunting program shot in the gut,
scurrying in a circle carrying the arrow
on a narrowing route. Funerals, parties,
and voyages greet the mind without gentleness.
Outside the mother blackbird shrieks. I can't help.

, , ,

In my final moment I'll sing a nonsense ditty
of reconciliation knowing that music came
before words. I'm only a painter in Lascaux.
I've sold my destiny for a simple quarter that bought
me the world that I've visited at twilight.

RETURN

Leaving on an exciting journey
is one thing, though most of all
I am engaged in homecoming—
the dogs, the glass of wine, a favorite
pillow that missed your head, the local
night with its familiar darkness.
The birds that ignored your absence
are singing at dawn assuring you
that all is inconceivable.

, , ,

I will sing even with my tongue sliced
into a fork. At the hospital this morning
I learned I'll be a nursemaid forever
or exactly as long as forever lasts. I study birds
that give me the tentative spaciousness of flight.

PRADO

After the ghostly Prado and in the Botanic
Gardens I tried to get in touch with Goya's
dogs. I called and called near the tiny blue roses
but likely my language was wrong
for these ancient creatures. Maybe they
know we destroyed the good hunting
in Spain and won't leave their paintings.
I can't give up. My waning vision
is fairly good at seeing dog souls. I wait
listening to unknown birds, noting the best voice
comes from one small and brown.
I feel a muzzle on my hand and knee
while thinking of the Caravaggio with David
looking down at the slain Goliath. This never
happens, this slaying of the brutal monster.
We know the ones that have cursed our lives.
Franco can't hear me talking to the ghost dog.
I was lucky that early on the birds and fish
disarmed me and the monster in my soul fled.
But where am I? Where can an animal hide?

DEATH AGAIN

Let's not get romantic or dismal about death.
Indeed it's our most unique act along with birth.
We must think of it as cooking breakfast,
it's that ordinary. Break two eggs into a bowl
or break a bowl into two eggs. Slip into a coffin
after the fluids have been drained, or better yet,
slide into the fire. Of course it's a little hard
to accept your last kiss, your last drink,
your last meal about which the condemned
can be quite particular as if there could be
a cheeseburger sent by God. A few lovers
sweep by the inner eye, but it's mostly a placid
lake at dawn, mist rising, a solitary loon
call, and staring into the still, opaque water.
We'll know as children again all that we are
destined to know, that the water is cold
and deep, and the sun penetrates only so far.

Jim Harrison, one of America's most versatile and celebrated writers, is the author of thirty-four books of poetry, fiction, and nonfiction — including *Legends of the Fall*, the acclaimed trilogy of novellas, and *The Shape of the Journey: New and Collected Poems*. His books have been translated into two dozen languages, and in 2007 he was elected to the American Academy of Arts and Letters. With a fondness for open space and anonymous thickets, he divides his time between Montana and southern Arizona.

Since 1972, Copper Canyon Press has fostered the work of emerging, established, and world-renowned poets for an expanding audience. The Press thrives with the generous patronage of readers, writers, booksellers, librarians, teachers, students, and funders — everyone who shares the belief that poetry is vital to language and living.

MAJOR SUPPORT HAS BEEN PROVIDED BY:

The Paul G. Allen Family Foundation

Amazon.com

Anonymous

Diana and Jay Broze

Beroz Ferrell & The Point, LLC

Golden Lasso, LLC

Gull Industries, Inc.
on behalf of William and Ruth True

Lannan Foundation

Rhoady and Jeanne Marie Lee

National Endowment for the Arts

Cynthia Lovelace Sears and Frank Buxton

Washington State Arts Commission

Charles and Barbara Wright

Special thanks are due to the following individuals for their generous support of this publication:

Anonymous

Bruce S. Kahn

Gregg Orr

Beef Torrey

To learn more about underwriting Copper Canyon Press titles,
please call 360-385-4925 x103

The Chinese character for poetry is made up of two parts: "word" and "temple." It also serves as pressmark for Copper Canyon Press.

Songs of Unreason is set in Adobe Jenson, a typeface based on metal type cut by Nicolas Jenson in fifteenth century Venice. "Suite of Unreason" is set in Legato, an original typeface by Evert Bloemsma. Book design and composition Valerie Brewster, Scribe Typography.